Dedication

To all the family, friends, colleagues, and strangers
who have blessed my life with their blessings.

Acknowledgments

This book grew out of a life experience and owes thanks
to many people along the way. My seminary classmates
who invited me to preach on the Sea of Galilee awakened the initial seed in me. The community from the
Come and See Conference in the Diocese of Cheyenne,
Wyoming, were the fertile soil in which the first
thoughts were planted. The numerous conferences and
retreats I was invited to direct shaped the thoughts and
enriched the ideas with insights from the many partici-
pants. The article on Beatitudes that was written for *U.S.
Catholic* provided sunshine in the surprising affirmation
it received from readers and the Associated Church
Press. Bayard/Twenty-Third Publications' enthusiasm for
a book and video combination made the whole project

seem possible, while the ongoing support of Gwen Costello and Mary Carol Kendzia saw the project through to completion. But none of it would have happened without the support of my husband, my family, and my friends, who prodded me to get it done, and the unfailing enthusiasm of our daughter Liz, who kept insisting it was her "favorite talk."

Contents

Introduction

The Vision

The tour boat made its way quietly across a fog-shrouded Sea of Galilee. The rain fell as mist, rather than droplets, clinging like dew to the plastic ponchos enveloping the few hardy souls who had remained on deck. Above us, the Mount of the Beatitudes hovered as the little ship dropped anchor. The gentle murmur of conversation rose from below deck, where the majority of the one hundred travelers had sought shelter. But outside, the sacred space had induced a reverent silence.

Each day of the tour had begun with a prayer service led by one of the ministers from one of the participating churches. Our seminary class had been asked to prepare for this day.

We were a motley crew. Only seven of the thirteen from our class were present, one Catholic priest, six ministers, and I, the lone lay person, lone woman in our group. When we had gathered to prepare a service focused on the beatitudes, the group had decided I should preach, since I was the only one who had never had that opportunity. It was the early 1980s and Catholic women were still under the edict of the apostle Paul to remain silent in church.

I was up most of the night preparing, but when I stood in the misty morning, holding the microphone that would carry my voice below deck, I knew we had gotten the text all wrong. Suddenly, I became deeply aware of Jesus looking out over the crowd who were poor, who were mourning and in need of comfort, who struggled for justice and still acted with mercy, the peacemakers, the pure of heart. His words were never meant as a challenge, they were a blessing, an acknowledgment of the presence of God in the people who had gathered on that hillside so many years ago. Jesus meant exactly what he said... "Blessed are you!"

As I began to speak, the sun found a tiny crack in the clouds, sending long fingers of light sparkling across the waters of the lake. Hesitantly, I offered the

> It was the message that discovered me.

words of comfort and blessing that found voice in me. It was not the text I had prepared, not the words that I had chosen to speak. It was the message that discovered me while the solitary rays of sunlight carved the words so deeply in my heart that the memory still takes my breath away. The inspiration of that moment twenty years ago was the beginning of this book.

As soon as I finished speaking, the misty rain resumed, prompting my colleagues to tease on every subsequent rainy day, "Let's get Kathy to preach."

At the end of that week, an elderly Baptist minister approached me in the praetorium in Jerusalem while the rest of the group was engaged in the morning prayer service. He was a tall, lanky man, an African-American Ichabod Crane, gentle and funny, and I had frequently sought the seat next to him on our long bus rides. He would work magic tricks and tell jokes, while his whole being emanated an aura of goodness. I had grown to love and admire him.

God never gives a gift for us to bury it, but surely there can be more than one way to use it.

Bending his head slightly to adapt his long body to the low ceilings, he explained softly that he had spent the whole week trying to find out who the woman minister was who had spoken on the Sea of Galilee. He was both surprised and delighted to discover it was his "seat mate" from the bus. He wanted to know "my church" so that he could come and listen to me preach some Sunday. It might be a long drive from his home in the Bronx, but he assured me it would be worth it. When I explained that I didn't exactly "have a church" in the way that he meant it, because "I'm Catholic," his eyes filled with tears. He took my face in his hands and looked deeply into my eyes. "Child," he said ever so gently, "Do you really think God would give you such a gift to bury it in the Catholic Church?"

I can still see his face, although I no longer remember his name. His words haunted me for years; his very goodness made them a challenge. I wondered if it was a prophetic calling. I knew it was true that God never gives a gift for us to bury it, but surely there can be more than one way to use it.

It was the word of God to the prophet Habbakuk that became my comfort and my guide: "Write the vision down, inscribe it on the tablets to be easily read...if it comes slowly, wait, for come it will, without fail" (Habakkuk 2:2–3). It was a vision whose time had not yet come.

I have written down the vision; I have inscribed it on the tablets. May you find in it the blessing it has been in my life.

The Love Song

Jesus stood on a mountainside
and looked out over the people.
They were hungry, and poor, sad and searching,
pure of heart and peacemakers.
And he blessed them.

Blessed are you poor in spirit,
    yours is the kingdom of God.
Blessed are you who mourn, you shall be comforted.
Blessed are you meek, for you shall inherit the earth.

Blessed are you who hunger and thirst for justice,
    you shall be satisfied.
Blessed are you merciful, you shall receive mercy.
Blessed are you pure of heart, you shall see God.
Blessed are you peacemakers,
    you shall be called the children of God.
Blessed are you who suffer persecution for justice
sake, yours is the kingdom of God.

—Matthew 5:1–10

We hear the beatitudes as another list of things to do. "You thought the commandments were tough, wait until you get to the beatitudes!" Down through the ages, we have memorized them, ignored them, examined our consciences by them, used them as our cry for social justice, and as the banner of Jesus' great reform, but never in that strange history have we ever paused long enough to simply celebrate them. I do not think Jesus was beginning a diatribe against materialism when he said "Blessed are you poor." I do not think it was political satire, sarcasm over the sorry state of Israel, as it has been played in some of the contemporary movies of Jesus. I do not think it was another list of commands. I think it was a blessing.

There is a god spark in everyone and in everything.

A blessing is the acknowledgment of the divine, of the holy, in the person or object or action being blessed. The Jewish people have blessings for everything, from parents and children, to earthquakes and tsunamis, to the humblest of bodily functions. No good Jew would ever use a blessing as a mandate; no good Jew would ever make a blessing conditional, "Blessed are you if...." A blessing was always a word of praise.

There is an ancient story from the heart of the Jewish mystical tradition, that Rachel Naomi Remen shares in her book *My Grandfather's Blessings: Stories of Strength, Refuge, and Belonging*: "At some point in the beginning of things, the Holy was broken up into countless sparks, which were scattered throughout the universe. There is a god spark in everyone and in everything, a sort of diaspora of goodness. God's immanent presence among us is encountered daily in the most simple, humble, and ordinary ways. The Kabbalah teaches that the Holy may speak to you from its many hidden places at any time. The world may whisper in your ear, or the spark of God in you may whisper in your heart....One is encouraged to acknowledge such unexpected meetings with the Holy by saying a blessing."

More traditional Judaism also affirms this concept of blessing. In *The Complete Book of Jewish Observance*, Leo Trepp says: "A Jew, partner in God's covenant, is called upon to make his or her life

> The holy may speak to you from its hidden places at any time.

authentic. He may not walk through his years routinely. He must develop *kavanah*, attunement, springing from an ever-renewed wonder at the work of creation and placing him in never-ending dialogue with God and the world....Not only are we called upon to be alert, but we must affirm the fact that we have seen and witnessed and absorbed the grandeur of creation, and we must do so in spoken words. This is *Berakhah*, the blessing."

Jesus was a good Jew. He knew the importance of blessing, of acknowledging each encounter with God. Isn't it possible that he looked out over the people, and in his own "never-ending dialogue with God," he witnessed the "grandeur of creation," the greatness of God, in them? Isn't it possible that as he looked into their eyes, he saw, in their beauty and their gifts the true beginnings of the reign of God? And he affirmed what he saw in spoken words, the *Berakhah*, the blessing.

Jesus came to establish the reign of God, in and through God's people. But God's people were also gifted

Blessing affirms the "god–life" in the one who is greeted.

and prepared with their own spark of the Holy to participate in the coming of that realm. By affirming that life in the people, by acknowledging it in blessing, Jesus called them to live their gifts in the reign of God.

"Blessed are you merciful—you who manifest the divine through the mercy you show to others; blessed are you who hunger and thirst for justice, who long for justice as some long for food...." Each blessing acknowledges a gift, a gift meant to be the breaking through of the divine in the human, in all of nature. Like the common Indian greeting, *Namaste*, "I see the divine spark in you," blessing affirms the "god-life" in the one who is greeted.

We often picture Jesus seated on the top of the mountain, but he probably walked among the people as he spoke, gently laying his hands on their heads. It would have been the way his parents blessed him every Sabbath evening, throughout his childhood. It would have been the natural thing to do.

Blessings also contained an orientation to the future, a promise of something yet to be. Like the blessing for rain that will bring forth grain from the soil, Jesus promises "...you shall receive mercy...you shall inherit the earth." This simple adherence to traditional form affirms the idea that Jesus truly meant his words as blessing.

Can you believe in me, the way that I believe in you?

We speak of "blessing" in contemporary language, as a surprising, gratuitous gift. I suspect this is much closer to the real meaning of Jesus' words. I think they were words of love for his people, his own particular love song. He is singing to them, and to us: "I love YOU, all of you, just the way you are. Can you believe in me, the way that I believe in you?"

It was the ultimate invitation to the people before him, and to all of us, to recognize our gifts and to allow our blessings to become the guiding principles for our lives.

Who were the "poor in spirit," the "meek," and "those who mourn" who were gathered on that hillside that day? This book is an attempt to walk through the life of Jesus, through the stories he told and the people he touched, and identify these "people of blessing." My hope is that each of their stories will cast new light on a particular beatitude, so that we might be better able to identify these gifts in ourselves.

The reader may disagree with many of my scriptural choices; I hope you will spend many hours poring over the gospels and coming up with better ones! The reader may disagree with many of my contemporary choices; I

> The beatitudes challenge me to discover and bless the spark of the Holy.

hope you will bring these blessings into your prayer life and name your own poor in spirit, meek, merciful, etc. I do not believe I have found THE ANSWER. I am simply trying to ask a bigger question.

More importantly, I am inviting you to discover the blessing in your own life. We live in a time of self-analysis. The Myers-Briggs tells me that I am an ENFP, which means I function best in a group, think best out loud, operate out of feelings and intuition, and have a great need to gather information. Dr. Gregorc tells me that I am a random concrete learner and function best when I am taught in a hands-on, creative situation. The Enneagram defines me as a "2," someone who needs to mother the world.

We certainly have all been given the opportunity to know how we function best, what our basic personality is, and what are its greatest flaws. But none of these tools begin with my giftedness.

The beatitudes begin with what is blessed about me and invite me into a self-knowledge and a life of prayer and service in keeping with the gift that I am. The beatitudes challenge me to discover and bless the spark of the Holy in everyone around me, to live in the awareness that I walk on holy ground.

2.

A Blessing of Gratitude

Blessed are the poor in spirit,
theirs is the kingdom of God.

His name was Lazarus. Not the brother of Martha and Mary, another Lazarus, perhaps a real person, but remembered only by the story Jesus told.

He was ill. Covered with sores. Like many of the poor of his day, he sat by the gates of the rich, waiting for the scraps

There is nothing intrinsically evil about being rich.

that fell from the rich man's table. But no scraps were given to him, and even the dogs came and licked his sores.

Time passed, and the poor man died and went to heaven, or the "bosom of Abraham," as the story tells it. The rich man also died and went to hell. Looking out from his torment and seeing Lazarus in the bosom of Abraham, the rich man begged Abraham to have God send someone back to his brothers to warn them (Luke 16:19–31).

～

"Blessed are the poor in spirit" is probably the most misunderstood of the eight beatitudes, and so it deserves a misunderstood parable and a misunderstood man as its champion.

This beatitude has been seen as a condemnation of materialism. Certainly, the gospel demonstrates a "special option for the poor." But when Jesus chose to condemn wealth, he did not mince words. "It is easier for a camel to pass through the eye of a needle than it is for a rich man to enter heaven" (Mark 10:25). Paragraphs later in this same sermon on the mount, he is going to tell his audience, "If your right hand causes you to sin, cut it off and cast it from you." Jesus was not known for being subtle. The assumption of subtlety here leads to a gross misreading of the word "blessed."

Lazarus did not merit heaven by being poor. There is nothing intrinsically evil about being rich, any more than there is anything intrinsically virtuous about being poor. I have known many holy wealthy people, and conversely, many evil paupers. The simple truth is that none of us merit salvation. It is a free gift.

> None of us merit salvation. It's a free gift.

The only thing necessary for salvation is the willingness to beg for it, then the openness to receive it as gift. I remember asking as a child, "If salvation is gift, what is the point in being good?" I was told that the way we lived our lives would determine our openness to the gift. Lazarus had spent his whole life begging. It was simple to ask one more time, easy to receive. Any comfort he had ever known had been undeserved gift and was accepted with gratitude.

The rich man, on the other hand, had always been in control. He created his own comfort; you can almost hear him saying he owed nothing to any man. He was a "self-made man" who was accustomed to getting what he wanted. He approached life with a sense of entitlement. He had worked hard; he deserved his reward. He did not know how to beg. He did not know how to ask for what

Generosity is all about us.

he needed, or even how to receive it as gift. And so he continued to try to control God, or at least Abraham, from beyond the grave. It was not his wealth that condemned him; it was his sense of entitlement, his inability to recognize everything as gift.

There was another rich man, a Roman centurion, who came to Jesus because his servant lay ill. The disciples had prepared Jesus. "This is a good man, he has supported the synagogue, he deserves to be heard." Jesus offered to go to the man's home to cure his servant. This man too was a man of power, accustomed to being obeyed. But he was poor in spirit, he knew that all is gift and he had no difficulty recognizing an authority even greater than his own. He asked nothing for himself, only for his servant. "Lord, I am not worthy that you should enter under my roof. Say but the word and my servant will be healed" (Matthew 8:5–13).

The poor in spirit are those who recognize the gift. Poor, like Lazarus, or rich, like the Roman centurion, they know they can never merit the thing they ask for, but they are unafraid to ask. Their prayer is simply "Lord, I am not worthy....I do not expect my prayer to be heard because I am good. I have the courage to ask, and the hope to expect, because You are good."

It is a misconception to believe that the poor in spirit are those who are generous. Generosity is all about us. We have enough to share and because we feel called to justice, or perhaps just because it feels good, we choose to share. We give out of our abundance. This is good and praiseworthy, but it is not poor in spirit.

> Giving is joy to them, not because they are generous, because they are grateful.

Poor in spirit is not about "giving until it hurts." Anyone can give until it hurts. You simply have to be incredibly stingy, and the first dime will hurt. We have all known people who appear to have so much, yet for them, parting with anything is agony.

The poor in spirit are those for whom it never hurts to give. We have known them, too. These are the people who will give you the shirt off their backs and make you feel like you are doing them a favor in taking it. The giving is joy to them, not because they are generous, because they are grateful. They recognize that everything they have in life is gift, and so they hold it with open hands.

Robert Wicks, in *Everyday Simplicity*, suggests that a sense of entitlement is one of the major enemies to a spiritual life. It hardens our souls. Yet, the answer, according to Wicks, is deceptively simple: receive, don't take.

Receive all as gift.

To be poor in spirit is to live with a consciousness of

Receive, don't take.

abundance. My granddaughter taught us all a lesson in abundance the Easter she was two and a half years old. It was the first year that she had any concept of Easter eggs, or bunny, or any of those delightful childhood rituals that accompany the feast. As the first grandchild, she had no older cousins or siblings to fill her with expectations.

We had hidden large plastic eggs filled with candy and small gifts all around the living-dining room area of our home. We presented her with a small basket and began the hunt with her. Once she realized what was in the eggs, she began searching in earnest. The basket was small and the eggs were large. It wasn't long before each additional egg would make the basket overflow. Every time that happened, she would stop to laugh delightedly and clap her hands.

Someone in the family suggested we simply provide a bigger basket. The other adults all chorused, "No!" emphatically. It was clear to us that the source of her joy was the overflow, the feeling of abundance the tiny basket was providing. It is easy to have more than enough if you keep your basket small. Little baskets produce a consciousness of abundance.

To live with the consciousness of abundance is to rejoice in the twelve baskets that were left over after the multitude

To be poor in spirit is to live with a consciousness of abundance.

was fed. To live without it is to wonder why there was no dessert.

Jesus told the story of a man who had an abundant harvest. He ordered that his barns be torn down and bigger ones built. Then he planned to eat, drink, and be merry. That night, God spoke to him saying, "Fool! This very night, your soul will be demanded of you" (Luke 12:16–21).

The problem was not the feasting; the problem was the bigger barns. The poor in spirit would have the feast, rejoicing in the overflow, sharing with anyone, regardless of need, simply for the joy of sharing. There would be nothing left for the bigger barns.

This joyful openhandedness is often manifested in a profound hospitality. There is always room in the homes and at the tables of the poor in spirit, no matter how limited space or food may be. It is a hospitality that has little to do with space and food and everything to do with, what the Irish call, "living in the shelter of one another." The poor in spirit do more than welcome people into their homes; they welcome people into the essence of who they are.

My younger daughter shared a brief encounter on the streets of New York City with a man who was truly poor in spirit. It was her freshman year of college and a mag-

The blessed poor in spirit walk through life with open hands.

...ical night in the city. The Christmas lights blinking in store windows, silver bells ringing in doorways, hot pretzels dominating the aromas of the street, all had combined to create the electrified atmosphere that is Christmas in New York.

After an evening of ice skating at Rockefeller Center, Liz and her friends were returning to the dorm, laughing and singing with the Christmas music that floated from the stores every time a door was opened. This was the city at its best and she was almost dancing down the sidewalk.

A man in his mid-thirties noticed her from across the street and jaywalked dangerously to intercept her path.

"You seem to be having a wonderful night," was his first comment.

"I am," she responded happily.

"Then, perhaps, you would have the answer to a very important question." He had fallen into step with the four girls, his eyes focused on Liz.

"I don't know. Try me," she responded.

"I need to know the secret of making a lot of money."

Liz stopped for a moment, looked up at him and said, with the certainty of an eighteen year old, "The secret is that you don't need a lot of money."

"But I do." He began to point out the problems of the city, the homeless, the AIDS epidemic, the lack of health care for the poor, the poverty of the children, the unemployment, and the crime. This was his city and he loved it. If he had a lot of money, he explained, there were so many programs he would institute, so much he could do to make the city better.

His impassioned speech continued as they walked, until they came to a corner where a woman sat begging, a tambourine in her lap. Without ever losing stride or interrupting his conversation, the man dumped all the money in his pockets into the tambourine and continued across the street. As they reached the opposite sidewalk, my daughter turned and looked up at him.

"I think you have found your answer," she said gently, "You just don't know it yet."

The blessed poor in spirit walk through life with open hands, ready to empty their pockets and their hearts, and give what they know they have been given.

Loving God, may the blessing of spiritual poverty envelop me. Give me a simple and grateful spirit that enables me to go through life with open hands, knowing that all I have and all I am is gift. Let gratitude transform me as it opens my spirit to the reign of God already among us.

3.

A Blessing of Compassion

Blessed are they who mourn,
for they shall be comforted.

T here was another man named Lazarus, a friend of
Jesus. He lived with his sisters, Martha and Mary,
and Jesus had often been welcomed into their
home. The well-worn story of Martha's complaint about
Mary refusing to help with the dinner preparations is far

"Where were you, Lord?"

more than a reflection on contemplative versus active lifestyles and ministries. It suggests a profound familiarity indicative of warm friendship.

And so, when Lazarus became ill, it was only natural that his sisters would send for Jesus. They had seen Jesus heal so many strangers, and Lazarus was his good friend. How could Jesus not come?

But he didn't come. When the word reached Jesus that Lazarus "whom he loved" was ill, he did not drop everything, even though the disciples had anticipated he would. He dilly-dallied around the countryside, and by the time he reached Bethany, Lazarus had already been dead for several days.

When word reached the house of Mary and Martha that the master was coming, Mary remained at home with the mourners. It was Martha who rushed to the edge of town, grief stricken and enraged with her friend who had let her down.

"Where were you, Lord? If only you had been here, my brother would not have died!"

These are not pleading words; they are angry, hurt words. Martha was mourning not only the death of her brother, but what she perceived as the death of her friendship with Jesus. She thought she was special. After

> "When we have the freedom to grieve, loss often turns naturally into compassion."

all, he had stayed at their home, eaten at their table. She thought he was her friend. But surely, if he had cared, he would have come.

And Jesus responds to her anguish with what sounds like a homily! "I am the resurrection and the life...." I wonder if she even heard the words. The question at the end of the speech penetrated her numbness and pain, "Do you believe?" She responds with the only answer she can give, "I believed in you. Where were you?" And Jesus was deeply moved (John 11:1–44).

❦

Martha is all of us. In the moment of tragedy, of pain, of death, the words that come from our hearts are "Where were you, Lord? I thought you loved me, I thought you cared."

Blessed mourners are the ones who are not afraid to voice the words, to cry out in rage at their own powerlessness and the mystery that is suffering and death. Jesus never called on us to "keep a stiff upper lip." Jesus said, "Blessed are they who mourn, for they shall be comforted." Out of that mourning, comes new life. Blessed mourners are those who deal honestly with the pain, and in the emptiness left behind, deep compassion is born.

"Grief is the way that loss heals."

In *My Grandfather's Blessings*, Rachel Naomi Remen says that "when we have the freedom to grieve, loss often turns naturally into compassion."

Dr. Remen offers a continuing education program for physicians who work intimately with death. Physicians in this country have been trained to repress their personal responses to the loss of a patient; getting involved is seen as unprofessional. Like so many of us, they have been taught to feel ashamed of weakness, to repress the pain, to "buck up," and move on. And so the pain remains, unrecognized and ungrieved, where it eats away at our souls. Dr. Remen says, "We have become numb, not because we don't care, but because we don't grieve. Grief is the way that loss heals."

When we find ourselves facing tragedy and grief, we turn to those who have also grieved, honestly and openly. Instinctively, we trust we will find compassion in those who have also endured tragedy, expressed their pain and rage, and found a way to go on living.

In the fall of 2001 when our nation was rocked by tragedy, our family faced its own personal grief. Three close family members were diagnosed with virulent, terminal cancers. The two women died within weeks of each other. The contrast of their deaths taught me much about mourning.

God is big enough to handle our rage.

We visited my sister-in-law shortly before her death. The room was filled with family when we arrived. Her husband and children stood on one side of the bed discussing animatedly the new chemotherapy that was going to be tried in the morning. As they shared the details with us, they kept turning to her for response, encouraging her that she could fight this, she could make it. Their "cheerleading" completely overwhelmed the quiet voice of the diminutive, elderly nun who stood on the other side of the bed reciting the litany of the dying.

My sister-in-law was young; my husband's brother had already lost one wife to cancer. He did not deserve this grief again, and I understood the desperate battle he was waging for her life. I felt torn between the battle on one side of the bed and the letting go on the other. I stood silently at the foot of the bed for several minutes. I made my decision as quietly and unobtrusively as possible, slipping next to the nun, responding softly to the litany.

I only had a few moments alone with my sister-in-law and I used them to tell her it would be okay to let go. It was okay to be angry. God is big enough to handle our rage. But God was waiting for her. She looked at me with eyes filled with fear and before I could say a word, the room had filled again with people. As we began our six-hour journey home, I asked my husband to call his brother and ask him to tell his wife it was okay to go home. I don't know if my brother-in-law ever told her. I only know Linda died that night.

There was something violent about our discussion in that hospital room. There was such outrage that this could be happening again, but even more so, there was a sense that we were all attempting to control this life. It left no room for the dying, no room for simply befriending the journey that was happening without us.

My cousin Eileen, roughly the same age as my sister-in-law, had won her first bout with cancer and had been keeping her multiple sclerosis at bay. But the liver cancer had proven to be too much for even her undaunted spirit. She spoke of death openly and calmly, and as we sat together planning her funeral, she told me she also had plans for heaven.

Eileen had had great difficulty bearing children. Her first child had been stillborn. Her second was transfused *in utero*. He was born with spina fida and other problems and survived only six days. Her third, a beautiful, healthy little boy, died of sudden infant death syndrome while she was at her father's wake. As soon as she got to heaven, Eileen explained, she was going to find her babies.

Blessed mourners do not rush in and try to fix us.

"And then," she said, "have I got words for God!"

I felt as if I were looking at Martha, standing on the edge of town, confronting Jesus. "Where were you, Lord?" I knew, at that moment, I had been privileged to love one of the truly "blessed mourners."

We find another group of blessed mourners at the foot of the cross. Like those women who stood with Mary, blessed mourners do not rush in and try to fix us. They stand by us, silently and steadfastly. They do not try to offer empty words or belittle our grief with placating remarks. They stand.

We can imagine them spending the sabbath with Mary, quietly bringing her tea and bread to keep up her strength. Jewish tradition required that a family in mourning do nothing for itself, not even light its own lamps. All was to be done by the community, and it is easy to understand at the foot of the cross who that community was. On the morning after the sabbath, while the disciples huddled frightened in an upper room, those same women returned to the grave to anoint the body of Jesus and prepare it for its journey. It is this steadfastness that was rewarded with the first news of the resurrection.

Blessed mourners help us to live our Holy Saturdays.

They enter into our grief and "abide with us."

My mother died in January of 2004, after a ten-year struggle with Alzheimers. At the moment of her death, it seemed like we had already been mourning for a long, long time. Three years earlier, I had written in my journal:

"I am not sure when we lost her. There was no tear-choked phone call to alert us. There was no stroke, no lingering moments as machines were turned off, no gathering at the bedside, no funeral rendition of 'Galway Bay' to mark the moment she passed.

"It happened silently, one lost thought at a time, like so many brilliant diamonds skittering across the frozen surface of her mind. Moments of forgetfulness stretched unnoticed into hours, the hours into days, and she was gone...(Dec. 1, 2001)."

I had been grieving for so long that I thought I was ready for her to leave. I was absolutely blindsided by the grief that enveloped me when her body succumbed to the flu. I felt orphaned, desolate, and so alone, despite the presence of my siblings, my own family, and their families. The constant reminder on every side that "It was for the best," made me want to scream at the people who were trying to comfort me. It wasn't for the best; it couldn't be. My mother was dead.

Only my husband's gentle presence restrained me

Blessed mourners come in all sizes.

from saying things I would probably still be regretting today. He absorbed my angry tirades and my tears each night, saying nothing, simply holding.

By the morning of the funeral, I felt as frozen as the January day itself. The music and scripture my Mom had loved, the voices of my own children proclaiming the readings and leading the singing, the presence of friends who had come a great distance to help, none of it seemed to penetrate the rigid ice that was keeping me upright.

Partway through the Mass, my two-year-old granddaughter reached for me, and my daughter lifted her gently into my arms. She wrapped one arm tightly around my neck and let her other hand rest softly on my wet cheek, wiping away the tears. Laying her head on my shoulder, she whispered "Nonni" several times, then curled up quietly in my arms. I remember the moment vividly, the warmth of her body, the smell of baby shampoo and soap, the unusual stillness that seemed to emanate from an intuitive empathy within her. It still comforts me.

Blessed mourners come in all sizes.

Compassionate God, grant me a respectful and compassionate spirit that stands steadfastly with those in pain, offering them comfort in their darkness. May their trust in me be a source of comfort and nourishment in my own life.

4.

A Blessing of Courage

Blessed are the meek, for they shall inherit the earth.

The incident happened in the region of Tyre and Sidon, north of Galilee, where, Matthew tells us, Jesus was traveling and teaching. He was probably not working miracles. There were few in the region from the house of Israel, and up until now, his true ministry had been limited to them. But his reputation had still gone before him. Crowds gathered, and a Canaanite woman, a foreigner, began following him, crying out, "Have mercy on me, Lord, Son of David; my daughter is tormented by a demon."

It is not hard to picture the scene: the large crowd, the teacher speaking gently, and the raucous woman following, continuing to interrupt, continuing to shout down those around her in her bid for attention. Jesus refused to respond, to even acknowledge her presence.

His rudeness has to have been hurtful. She had been told he was the gentlest of men; he would care about her daughter's suffering. Perhaps she had come because she had heard him before and had lingered on the edges of the crowd as he healed others. He had to listen. She cried out again.

Frustrated by her persistence, the disciples approached Jesus and asked him to send her away. She was destroying the mood; she was annoying everyone. But Jesus would not even deign to speak to her. Instead, he explained to his apostles, that he had only come for the lost sheep of the house of Israel. This woman didn't qualify for his aid, or even, it seemed, for his attention.

Undaunted, the woman forced her way through the crowd and knelt down in front of him, pleading, "Lord, help me." She had left him no choice; he had to speak to

"Woman, great is your faith."

her now. And so Jesus spoke, hurtful words, one of his harshest responses in the whole of scripture. "It is not fair to take the children's food and throw it to the dogs."

He had called her "a dog." This hurting woman had only wanted help for her daughter, and the great, holy man had called her a dog. In the presence of all of her friends and neighbors, he had called her a dog. In the presence of dignitaries from town who had also come out to hear him, he had called her a dog. It should have been enough to send her slinking away, broken and humiliated.

But this was a woman who had nothing to lose. She had no power, no status to defend, no social position. This is true meekness. It is the courage to speak the truth from a position of powerlessness. And so she challenged Jesus.

"Yes, Lord, it is fair, for even the dogs eat the crumbs that fall from the Master's table." Basically, she is telling Jesus that he is wrong, that he has misunderstood his own ministry. "You are called to more, much more than you originally thought. Open your heart and your mind to where your God is calling you."

At that moment, a truly amazing thing happened: Jesus changed his mind! He looked down at the woman still obstructing his path, still on her knees, and, I suspect, helped her to her feet. He was about to pay her the greatest compliment he had to give; he would have wanted her standing. "Woman, great is your faith." And then he promised her that her daughter had been healed (Matthew 15:21–28).

> The courage to speak the truth from a position of powerlessness.

Only twice does scripture show us a Jesus who rethinks his position on something. Only twice do we see him changing his mind. Both times, the issue was the scope of his own ministry. Both times, he was confronted by a meek woman.

The other situation wasn't critical. There was no dying child; just a bride and groom who might have been embarrassed. And another meek woman intervened on their behalf: "Son, they have no wine." "What is it to us? My time has not yet come." Again, the response seems unnecessarily harsh, especially when the gospel points out that he addressed his own mother as "Woman." But Mary simply ignored his words, telling the waiters to follow his instruction. She might as well have said to Jesus, "Get over yourself!" And Jesus discovered his time had indeed come (John 2:1–12).

≈

Meekness. It is probably the beatitude we like least. Certainly, the idea of meekness is less than appealing. Years

True meekness is the courage and freedom of the person who has nothing to lose.

ago, in preparation for a talk on the beatitudes, I looked up "meek" in a large thesaurus. Almost all the synonyms were pejorative. "Overly submissive, passive, wishy-washy." Is this meekness? Did Jesus mean "Blessed are the wishy-washy"? "Blessed are the doormats, for they shall be walked upon"?

The Canaanite woman and Mary the mother of Jesus teach us about true meekness. True meekness is the courage and freedom of the person who has nothing to lose: Martin Luther King, Jr., on the steps of the Lincoln Memorial awakening all of us to his dream; Gandhi leading his march to the sea, claiming for his people what had become a symbol of their oppression; Sister Theresa Kane asking John Paul II to reconsider the call of women to priesthood. Meekness is the courage that speaks out when speaking out is social suicide. Meekness is the courage that stands its ground when the odds are hopelessly stacked against us. Those with the blessing of meekness are the ones who are not afraid to speak the truth to power.

When Jesus stood before Pilate, Pilate held all the power. Yet it was Pilate who was bound and tormented

> Meekness is
> the courage
> that speaks out
> when speaking
> out is social
> suicide.

by the situation, Pilate who tried to make a public ritual of freeing himself from the responsibility for his own actions, Pilate who probably never slept peacefully again.

In *Called to Question: A Spiritual Memoir*, Joan Chittister makes this observation about powerlessness. She defines it as "Power for"; it could easily be defined as meekness.

"In the end power does not lie in wealth and authority; it lies in having nothing to lose. When we have nothing to lose or to gain in a situation, we are finally free. Then, the only things that stand between us and integrity are consciousness and truth. Powerlessness does not neutralize us; it drives us on. We are the only ones on the battlefields of life with an eye on the questions alone. Everybody else is too busy calculating the effect of the loss of the situation on their reputations and their careers and their images and their positions. The powerless go naked into combat and cannot be scarred. They alone have the power to endure it all."

The meek are our prophets. Like the prophets of old, they stand outside the gates of the city, outside the gates of our institutions and governments, challenging us out of our complacency, our safe ruts. On those rare occasions where their authenticity and integrity lead them into positions of authority, the challenge is to remain true to themselves, to challenge even the authority they have been given.

One of those rare people was Thurgood Marshall, the Supreme Court's first black justice, the former lawyer who had successfully argued the Brown vs. the Board of Education school-desegregation decision. Writing of him in her 2003 memoir, *The Majesty of the Law: Reflections of a Supreme Court Justice,* Sandra Day O'Connor speaks of his gift:

"Although all of us come to the court with our own personal histories and experiences, Justice Marshall brought a special perspective. His was the eye of a lawyer who saw the deepest wounds in the social fabric and used law to help heal them. His was the ear of a counselor who understood the vulnerabilities of the accused and established safeguards for their protection. His was the mouth of a man who knew the anguish of the silenced and gave them a voice."

Some might argue his was the blessing of justice, but it was more than the acute awareness of need that obligated him to act. It was his own experience of the powerlessness of his people that compelled him to speak out. It is hard to believe he would have remained quiet regardless of winning or losing, regardless of acceptance or rejection.

In my own life, the person who showed me the courage inherent in meekness was Bernard Haring.

> The powerlessness of his people compelled him to speak out.

Father Haring was a noted moral theologian, one of the best our church has known. He was also a deeply holy man. We, his students in the summer graduate theology program, all knew that he was holy because we felt holy when we were with him.

It was the mid 1970s and the church was still awash with the furor raised by *Humanae Vitae*. Charles Curran was under investigation by the Holy Office for his teaching on the subject, and Father Haring had been vocal in both his support of Curran and his insistence on the primacy of individual conscience. We walked through picket lines on our way to class each day, peopled by conservative Catholic groups and newspaper reporters, looking for inflammatory quotes.

When Father Haring finally granted one interview, he articulated his own stand clearly, with little concern for repercussions. However, the story that hit the news was a dreadful distortion of his words. We were infuriated. We offered to petition for a second interview, to offer a rebuttal, to do something to protect his name and his

> "It is the
> decision not
> to be passive,
> not to be
> a victim."

teaching. He refused simply, smiling placidly. "I have spoken the truth. The truth cannot hurt me. I have nothing left to say."

When I had my oral examination with him, which was little more than a pleasant, personal interview, I asked him how long it had taken him to stop being afraid, to develop the unflappable gentleness that has no need to strike back or defend. He smiled knowingly and said, "It is taking my lifetime."

In *Writing in the Dust: After September 11*, Rowan Williams redefines pacifism in a way that I think captures the essence of meekness. "It is the decision not to be passive, not to be a victim, but equally not to avoid passivity by reproducing the violence that has been done to you....It requires courage and imagination." Certainly, the Canaanite woman had both. Courage is not the opposite of fear. Courage is the child of fear, often born in powerlessness. Nurtured with anger, it can become violence; nurtured with integrity, it becomes meekness.

In *Scarred by Struggle, Transformed by Hope*, Joan Chittister says, "Courage does not come in a burst of insight. Courage comes out of the way we think and the way we live from Sunday to Sunday, every week of our lives." She insists that "the real spiritual question is not,

Do I have the power to change this? The real spiritual question is, Do I have the courage to say no to it?"

Meekness speaks out of its integrity. Meekness speaks out of its vulnerability. Meekness speaks out of its anguish. Meekness speaks out.

God of courage, let the blessing of meekness be upon me. Give me a gentle and inclusive spirit that reaches out with courage to the marginalized. Help me to give voice to my own powerlessness, that it might stand as a sign of contradiction to all who would abuse authority.

A Blessing of Justice

Blessed are they who hunger and thirst for justice,
for they shall be satisfied.

There is a little boy who appears only in the gospel
of John. While the synoptics all tell a similar
story, only John's account includes his presence.
Jesus had been preaching and a large crowd had followed
him. By meal time, they were far from their homes and far

from the neighboring villages. As they approached, Jesus asked Philip where they would buy bread for so many. Philip, bewildered by the implication that they were somehow responsible for feeding this mass of people, responded that it would cost a fortune to accomplish the task.

> Justice is a blessing that will not let us eat lunch while the person next to us goes hungry.

At this moment, John tells us, a small boy approached Andrew with five loaves and two fish. Unlike Philip, this child did feel responsible for the hunger of the group. He could not have been all that young; he would not have been out in the hills alone. I doubt that he was naïve enough to believe five loaves and two fish could feed the multitude. And I think we can be reasonably sure that he was not theologically astute enough to have any idea of what Jesus might do with his offering. It did not matter that he did not have enough. He simply could not eat his own lunch while anyone else went hungry (John 6:1–15).

~

This is the blessing of justice. All of us are called to do justice; the gospel message is clear in this regard. But the blessing of justice is more than this. The blessing of justice is the painful awareness that does not leave us free to enjoy our own comfort while others are suffering; it is a blessing that

> "God does not ask us to be successful, God asks us to be faithful."

will not let us eat lunch while the person next to us goes hungry.

For several years, until pregnancy and a baby made the job too dangerous, our middle child worked in an inner-city program for at-risk youth. Most of the teenagers she worked with were suffering from drug addiction. They had been placed in the program by the court system. It was the last stop before detention, or what was once known as reform school.

The young people who came to the program were usually in it for six weeks to three months. Then they would return to the streets. Often, within days, they would be back in the courts. The recidivism rate for teenage drug addiction in the United States is 97%. I once asked my daughter how she could continue in a job that had to be so incredibly discouraging.

"How can you do this?" I had asked.

She looked at me, a little bewildered, and said, "Mom, how can I not do this?"

This is the blessing of justice, the hunger and thirst for justice. We responded to the needs our daughter brought home to us, giving money and assistance in whatever ways we could manage. That is the justice that the gospel calls us all to. But ours was not the awareness that kept our daughter on the streets with her teens. Hers is the blessing of justice.

I shouldn't have been surprised. During high school, this same daughter had insisted that we switch to cloth napkins when she discovered how paper mills were deforesting the Northwest. It did not matter that the amount of paper in the napkins of a lifetime in our family would probably not make a dent in the forest; it mattered that we cared and that we did what we could.

Mother Teresa often told the story of her journeying through Calcutta by train and being overwhelmed with grief at the plight of the dying poor. She left her own religious order and began the work that made her name a household word all over the world. Time and time again, she told reporters who pointed out the limits of what she was able to do about the situation, "God does not ask us to be successful, God asks us to be faithful." It did not matter if she could only reach a small percentage of those dying in the streets. For the ones she did reach, her presence made a profound difference.

There is a story that has been circulating on the internet for several years. I am sure anyone who is online at all has come across it at least once. But I am still going to risk repeating it here. For me, it is the essence of those called to do justice.

A violent storm, followed by a particularly low tide, had left thousands of starfish stranded along miles of seacoast. An old man walked slowly along the water's edge, stooping to pick up an occasional starfish and throw it back into the sea.

A young man, jogging along the beach, stopped and watched for a moment, then laughingly asked, "What are you doing, old man? Look at the thousands of starfish on the sand in front of you. What you are doing can't possibly make a difference."

The old man was silent and continued picking up one starfish at a time. The jogger resumed his run, heading down the beach laughing and shaking his head. As the old man threw one more fish into the water, he said softly, "It matters to this one."

When Paul VI awakened us as a church to the concept of a "faith that does justice," peace and justice groups sprang up in parishes and dioceses all over our country. It was the late 1960s. The civil rights movement and the War on Poverty were turning many people who considered themselves ordinary citizens into social activists, while the war in Vietnam was turning people who considered themselves patriots into pacifists.

As a child growing up in the fifties, my parents had taken me to Washington, DC, where I had seen my first

"Black Crow" signs on motels. When my mother explained that those motels were for the "Negroes," I asked why they didn't want to stay with us. This was not prejudice, it was ignorance.

> The sixties destroyed any innocence that might have been part of our ignorance.

The sixties destroyed any innocence that might have been part of our ignorance. It made us culpable for centuries of abuse. It was a spiritual and political awakening to prejudices so deeply ingrained we did not even know they existed.

With the awakening came rage: anger at our own powerlessness, anger at the systems that had abused us, anger that we had been part of systems abusing others. Riots erupted all across the United States until several of our cities had become bombed out shells, smoldering monuments to the anger of powerless people.

In the midst of the chaos, there were those who continued to work quietly for change. Job corps volunteers in a hundred different cities found work for the unemployed. People from all over the country marched peacefully to Selma, refusing to respond violently to police brutality along the way. A handful of courageous African-American children walked into white educational enclaves and a handful of equally courageous Caucasian

> **"The hardest thing in the world is to know how to act so as to make the difference that can be made..."**

students reached out in friendship.

"The hardest thing in the world is to know how to act so as to make the difference that can be made; to know how and why that differs from the act that only releases or expresses the basic impotence of resentment." These are the words of Rowan Williams, responding to the challenge of September 11. In his response, he offered one of the best definitions I have found of justice. "It is about trying to act so that something might possibly change, as opposed to acting so as to persuade ourselves that we're not powerless."

The meek challenge the system that victimizes; the just care for the victims. Gandhi and Mother Teresa cared for the same community. Gandhi's gift was one of meekness. Mother Teresa's was one of justice.

The just live lives characterized by service to life as they find it, and to life as it finds them. They act to make "the difference that can be made."

Rachel Naomi Remen says: "True service is not a relationship between an expert and a problem; it is far more genuine than that. It is a relationship between two people who bring the full resources of their combined humanity to the table and share them generously."

To do this requires a profound gift of awareness, awareness of both the hungry people around us and the loaves and fish in our own basket.

God of Justice, awaken my spirit to the needs of those around me. Keep me faithful to the tasks that integrity compels me to accomplish. Though I will never satisfy the hunger of the earth, bless my efforts so that they satisfy the hunger of my own heart.

6.

A Blessing of Mercy

Blessed are the merciful,
for they shall receive mercy.

I t is the story within the story, the story we don't get
to hear. We all know the story of the prodigal son
who demanded his inheritance, left his home, went
to a foreign land, and squandered his money. In the end,
he finds himself feeding the pigs on someone else's farm

and realizes that the servants in his father's house are better fed than he is. He decides to go home, not because he is sorrowful, but, quite simply, because he is hungry. The

> God's forgiveness comes first, even before we are sorry.

whole way home, he is rehearsing what he will say. His speech is somewhat reminiscent of the ones I remember rehearsing before Saturday night confessions in a pre-Vatican II church. "Father, I have sinned against heaven and you, I am not worthy to be called your son." Still, not a word about being sorry!

The father is walking the road, waiting for him. He greets him with open arms, forgiving him before the son has a chance to say a word. He calls for a robe to clothe his son, a ring for his finger, and a party to celebrate (Luke 15:11–32).

~

We tend to miss the point. It is a story about God's loving forgiveness of us. We are not the father in this story; God is. It is a story about how God's forgiveness comes first, even before we are sorry. It is God's forgiveness that draws us home, God's forgiveness that meets us on the road and welcomes us. If we have a "firm purpose of amendment," it is only because we have already been forgiven. Conversion is inspired by forgiveness; it was never a condition for God's forgiveness. We are not the father. We are the prodigal, or perhaps, even more likely, we are the elder brothers.

It is his story, the story within the story, that we often overlook or misunderstand. After the younger son left, have you ever really thought about who took over all his work on the farm? The elder brother. When the grieving father lost interest in the land and began to walk the road searching for his son, who took over all the father's work? The elder brother. And when the mother wept at night for her baby that was lost, who awoke, made her a cup of tea and sat with her in the darkness? The elder brother.

He watched his parents grow old, prematurely aged by grief and stress. He watched his home grow dark, as if the joy had somehow been extinguished when his brother left. He watched his own inheritance become rundown as he struggled to do the work of three.

And so the elder brother was not home when the prodigal arrived. He was out in the fields; it had become necessary to work late to finish the work his brother's and father's absences had left undone.

It is not hard to picture him returning home, long after the sun is down, exhausted and dirty from his day in the fields. The light from the house and the noise of the gathering greeted him long before he reached the doorway. There was obviously a party going on. Laughter and music assaulted him as he approached. What had happened that had changed things so radically? There had not been a party in his home in years!

"I bet he thought the party was for him. "

I was telling the elder brother's story to a group of young families. I had asked them to walk the journey in the elder brother's shoes. As we pictured him approaching the house, a young teenager volunteered, "I bet he thought the party was for him. His parents finally woke up (you know, the way people seem to do after they've been grieving and kind of out of it for a long, long time) and they realized all he had been doing. He might have thought it was a surprise party to say 'Thank-you'."

Whatever he thought, he was probably not expecting what the servant told him. "Your brother has returned and your father has killed the fatted calf to welcome him."

I have often wondered why Jesus mentioned the calf. Who was fattening up the calf? Probably the elder brother. He was the only one caring for the farm. Perhaps the calf was for himself. The fact that he complained specifically about it would indicate it had great importance. Perhaps, he had been waiting for his parents to awake from their fog of grief and arrange a wedding for him. He would have been ready. He would have been able to

> Justice grants people their due. Mercy grants them what they do not deserve and could not earn.

tell them he had fattened the calf for the feast.

Whatever the reason, the fatted calf was the last straw. It was adding insult to injury. The elder brother was furious! What one of us wouldn't have been? He didn't want to go into the party, and I must admit, my sympathies are all with him.

The father left his guests and his younger son, and came out to the elder brother. I suspect his words to his son are some of the most misunderstood, misinterpreted in scripture. He said, "Son, all that I have is yours." This is the part we got wrong. He was not talking about the farm! The farm already belonged to the elder son. He was the only heir left; the other son had already taken his inheritance.

The father was talking about his forgiveness. I believe he is saying, "I understand. I know the hurt is too deep, the pain too great right now for you to forgive. I have enough forgiveness for both of us! I will understand if you can't forgive yet. But your brother that was lost is found and you need to come into the party. You need to act with mercy" (Luke 15:11–32).

Justice grants people their due. Mercy grants them

what they do not deserve and could not earn. Mercy is beyond forgiveness. It is what we give to the person we cannot forgive, the one who has no claim on our forgiveness. When the governor gives a stay of execution, we call it an act of mercy. We are not condoning the actions of the criminal; we are choosing to act with mercy.

The merciful are often those who have been wounded so deeply they don't know if they can ever forgive, and yet, they choose to act with kindness. They refuse to let their actions be governed by their own anger and pain.

Did the elder brother go inside to the party? The story doesn't tell us. Like most parables, it calls us to decide what we are going to do by not providing the answer to the obvious question. But I have to believe in the elder brother. He has stood by his parents through all of their grief; it is difficult to imagine that he would hurt them in that moment. It would violate his own integrity and faithfulness.

I met a man on the lecture circuit; our paths crossed at a couple of catechetical conventions in the western United States. I think he had been a lawyer before his daughter was murdered at Columbine High School. He had left his profession and was devoting his time to traveling around the country speaking out against the death penalty. I spoke with him briefly in a hotel lobby outside of Reno, Nevada. I was struggling with a huge issue of

> "An eye for an eye and a tooth for a tooth: the quickest route to a toothless, sightless world."

forgiveness in my own life, and I asked if he had been able to forgive the two boys who had staged the assault. He answered slowly and thoughtfully that he was not sure. He only knew that if we responded to violence with violence, we would be feeding the violence and building a more violent world.

His answer reminded me of a definition I saw years ago in a little book called *The Singer*. "Definition: An eye for an eye and a tooth for a tooth: the quickest route to a toothless, sightless world."

The merciful are those who choose to act with mercy, to do the kind and compassionate thing, regardless of whether or not they are able to forgive. It is often a hard-won choice and this wounded father possessed a profound dignity, a peaceful aura, that I suspect is a hallmark of the merciful.

When Darwin first developed his evolutionary "survival of the fittest" paradigm, he could find no basis for "mercy" in nature. In an article in *Commonweal* (June 17, 2005), Peter Quinn wrote: "The concept of an emotion unrelated to self-interest, of an impulse to mercy that overrides notions of utility or fitness, is hard to place in this scientific equation."

The presence of mercy, and of the merciful among us,

gives silent testimony to the fact that we are more than the physical genetics that make up our mental and physical beings.

There has been a short story making the internet rounds over the last two years that captures the essence of the merciful.

> Mercy gives testimony to the fact that we are more than the physical genetics.

A Native-American chief was telling his grandson a story. "Child, in the heart of every person are two great wolves, waging war with each other. One wolf is the wolf of hatred, revenge, and anger. The other wolf is the beast of kindness, gentleness, and compassion. The battle is constant and fierce, without interruption."

"But Grandfather," the child responded, "which wolf wins?"

His grandfather spoke gently. "Whichever wolf the person chooses to feed."

In writing about the Twin Tower tragedy, Rowan Williams makes this observation:

"I am spoken to; I have some choices about how I answer....Violence is a communication, after all, of hatred, fear, or contempt, and I have a choice about the language I am going to use to respond. If I decide to answer in the same terms, that is how the conversation will continue."

Forgiveness is the gift.... Mercy is the decision.

The man I met in Reno had decided on his language. He had decided which wolf to feed.

I remember being told during a marriage encounter back in 1973, that love is not a feeling, it is a decision. We make that decision every time we do the loving thing. I never completely agreed with that statement. Love is certainly more than a feeling, but, in my life, it has also been much more than a decision. Love is a gift. Deciding to do the loving thing may open us to receive the gift and deepen the gift already present, but it is not quite the same thing.

I suspect the same relationship exists between forgiveness and mercy. Forgiveness is the gift. Sometimes, no matter how firmly we decide to forgive, in our heart of hearts we know it hasn't happened. Something reminds us of the hurt, touches the raw spot within, and the old pain and anger bubble to the surface. At that moment, the prodigal Father/Mother promises: "All that I have is yours. Just come to the party."

Mercy is the decision.

Merciful God, fill me with the tenderhearted
goodness that speaks the language of gentleness
in the face of violence, the language of love
in the face of rejection. Open my heart
to your forgiveness when I am unable to forgive,
and let my actions be a sign to others
of your merciful love.

7.

A Blessing of Truth

Blessed are the pure of heart, for they shall see God.

He was an old man who had been waiting a life-time for the salvation of Israel. Not a priest, not a pharisee, just an ordinary elderly lay man, and God had promised that he would not die without seeing the salvation he longed for. When he awoke that morn-ing it was to a profound sense of the presence of God. This would be the day!

> They both
> sensed the
> extraordinary
> nature of this
> moment.

The temple courtyard was crowded. A massive area, the size of several football fields, was filled on this morning with the usual trappings of religion. The pharisees and their disciples were sitting or walking in groups, discussing the prophets, the writings, the signs of the coming Messiah. The salesmen were hawking their animals for the sacrifices, while the rams, oxen, and turtle doves filled the area with their own noise and their own particular smells. The money changers were set up alongside them, exchanging coins for the foreigners and gossip with their colleagues. The priests walked silently through the throng, heading for the holy of holies and the sacrificial duties of the day.

And then there were the worshipers, rich and poor, young and old, stopping with the money changers to get the coin of the realm, then searching for animals for their necessary sacrifices. As Simeon wended his way across the busy courtyard, he caught sight of Anna and moved toward her. She was even older than he was and he never remembered a day when he had not found her praying in the temple.

Today, however, they hesitated at the edge of the courtyard at the temple entrance. It required no words between

Anna and Simeon looked into the eyes of that baby, and they saw God.

them; they both sensed the extraordinary nature of this moment.

Into the middle of the melee came one more couple bearing an infant son. The mother had come to offer the required sacrifice for purification. As they walked across the courtyard, all that the money changers saw was another poor couple carrying another poor baby. As they bought the turtle doves for the sacrifice, all the seller saw was another poor couple. And as they entered the temple, all that the learned pharisees, scribes, and priests saw was another poor couple with another poor baby.

Anna and Simeon looked into the eyes of that baby, and they saw God (Luke 2:22–38).

~~~

So often, we are fooled by appearances. We cannot get beyond what is on the outside to see what is on the inside. The priests, the scribes, the pharisees had all the information they needed to recognize the Messiah; they simply could not see beyond the simple human trappings they had not expected.

The promise at the end of this beatitude is actually the result of being pure of heart. The pure of heart refuse to be blinded by the external casing. Therefore, the pure of heart see God. The spark of the Holy that the *Kabbalah* teaches is in all of us is, visible to the pure of heart.

> The pure of heart refuse to be blinded by the external casing.

In John's gospel, we find another man who was pure of heart. We don't know his name; we only know he was blind. As Jesus approached him sitting by the side of the road, the disciples began to ask, "Who sinned, this man or his parents?"

This man had probably been sitting by the side of the road begging for years. In a society where disability was seen as the result of evil, the disabled had no other choice except to beg if they hoped to survive. He was a fixture to his friends and neighbors. He had often heard itinerant rabbis arguing this same question with their disciples, "Who sinned?" In the past, there may have even been a time when he wondered about the answer, when he asked the rabbi what kind of a God would have done this to him. But he had given up asking.

On this day, he ignored the conversation and held out his hand. Jesus approached, and without ever speaking to the man, spat on the ground, put mud on the man's eyes, and told him to go and wash in the pool of Siloam.

Have you ever known someone who is blind? If so, you will know there has to be more to the story than John tells us at this point. My three-year-old niece has

The blind man saw what everyone else was too blind to see.

been blind from birth. No stranger could ever approach her and start to put something on her face. She would fight and scream and resist, and she has known nothing but love and gentleness in her short life.

This beggar had spent his whole life maligned as a sinner, probably jeered at and ridiculed, maybe even spat upon. The sound of a man spitting would have been no surprise, but the mud had to have been!

Something happened at that moment that moved the blind man to let Jesus touch him. I suspect, in that instant, the blind man saw what everyone else was too blind to see. The blind man saw God. Perhaps it was similar to the sensation we have when we are resting outside with our eyes closed and the sun suddenly peeps out from behind a cloud. Through closed eyes, we see the brightness. We feel the warmth on our faces, and we recognize the sun.

This man who was blind saw the radiance that Peter, James, and John had witnessed on Mount Tabor. He felt the warmth on his face, the sudden presence of the sun in his own personal darkness. He saw a brilliance that those around him failed to recognize. He went to the pool and washed, and he saw God.

The disciples, blinded by ancient prejudice, could not see the man, only a person they thought was a sinner. The neighbors, blinded by their limited expectations ("our neighbor is blind and this man can see"), could not see the miracle. How often all of us are confronted with something "too good to be true" and we simply do not accept the miracle our eyes tells us we are seeing.

> There are none so blind as those blinded by religion.

The man's parents, blinded by their fear of being tossed out of the synagogue, simply refused to acknowledge what they could not help but see. And the pharisees, blinded by religion, refused to see what was right in front of them. "This man could not be from God because he broke God's law by healing on the Sabbath." There are none so blind as those blinded by religion.

Only the blind man was pure of heart; only the blind man saw God (John 9:1–41).

Our younger daughter, Liz, is pure of heart. Even as a young child, her descriptions of people she met were surprisingly free of outward attributes and focused on inner qualities. Age, race, physical attractiveness were all incidental. She had trouble recalling them if asked, and my husband and I decided early on not to ask. We did not want to threaten her vision of things. This became increasingly evident as she grew older, moved beyond the family and neighborhood, and we saw less of the new friends she met. When she left home for college at New York University, I found myself struggling to picture the people she described, and often being startled to eventually learn we were discussing an eight year old she had spoken to on the swings in the park or an old woman begging on the streets.

Her first weeks in the city were incredibly lonely. For someone who normally makes friends easily, she found the separation from family and home surprisingly difficult, and the ills of the city surrounding her somewhat overwhelming. Until she made a friend who taught her to play chess.

In typical Liz fashion, she told me nothing about appearance, age, etc., and everything about his philosophical stance on world issues and the problems of the city, his insights on college, his thoughts about home. I decided he had to be an upper classman; no freshman could have achieved this much wisdom. He seemed to be able to drain away much of her initial anxiety and frustration as she absorbed his chess lessons. He encouraged her to call home, to stay close to her parents. Without ever having met this man, I was growing to love him.

Early one Sunday morning, before dawn had actually

broken, Liz called home feeling much in need of some Mom time. I hopped on a bus and made it to the city by 8:30 AM. Greeting me at the subway station, Liz asked what I wanted to do for the day. "Meet the amazing chess man, if you think he is up." (Liz was our third child in college and I was well aware of the sleeping habits of the species.)

Liz assured me it would be easy to check. We headed toward Washington Square, surrounded by the still-sleeping Sunday morning city. The homeless clustered on doorsteps, huddled under makeshift blankets, chilled in the late October air. The park was silent, with more homeless on every bench. Their presence had been a big part of Liz's anguish when she first arrived in the city. Early in September I had counseled my weeping daughter that she did not have the power to change the situation, but she could help by choosing to do one thing and doing it faithfully. We had not talked about it since.

As we headed through the park, I assumed we were taking a shortcut to 8th Avenue, where Liz's dorm was located. We stopped at a park bench beside an elderly man with sleep still lingering in the air around him. His eyes lit up as they fell on my daughter and she rushed to greet him and introduce me. Here was the chess wizard, the man who had befriended my daughter through her

lonely, difficult first weeks of college. He was quite elderly, homeless, and his accent and dark skin suggested
Jamaica. My daughter had watched him playing chess in
the park one day, and sensing her loneliness, he had
reached out and befriended her. I might not have even
seen him, if I had not seen him first through my daughter's eyes. I would have missed meeting and loving a
beautiful man.

After a brief conversation, Liz decided to "walk" me
through her typical day. Pointing out the library, which
towers over Washington Square, she explained that her
day actually began at 2:00 AM when the library closed
and she finished studying. I looked around at the Square,
knowing well its reputation for drug traffic, seeing the
homeless, and those who had been too drunk or stoned
to make it home, asleep on its benches, and pictured my
seventeen-year-old traversing its paths at 2:00 AM.

Not wanting to frighten her, but terribly frightened
myself, I asked how many of her friends usually studied
late. She laughed. No one had to study as much as she
did. She was the only one still up at that hour.

I thought about our rural town where they rolled up
the sidewalks at 6:00 PM and wondered how to address
my daughter's unwary innocence without destroying her.

We continued on, past her dorm, down the street

toward the building where her first morning class took place. The NYU campus is spread out among various city buildings purchased by the university, interspersed with businesses along the city streets. As we walked, she chattered happily while I glanced fearfully at the poor and derelict of the city spread out on its doorsteps.

She stopped at her favorite coffee shop with the simple remark, "I always stop here in the morning." As we stepped over the man sleeping in the entrance way and entered the shop, everyone greeted her by name. It was "vintage Liz" to have established herself so firmly in one quarter of this huge city. The waitress rushed by our booth asking, "The usual?" "Yes, and one for my Mom." "Hi, Mom!" the waitress called over her shoulder, moving at New York speed, returning quickly with two hot chocolates.

"So this is your Mom?" "Yes, I'm showing her my world." My daughter's level of comfort was tangible and I struggled with weighing my fears for her against this newfound sense of "home."

By the time we finished our hot chocolate, I still had not decided what to do. We moved toward the cashier and my daughter said, "My treat, Mom." As she placed the money on the counter, the waitress said apologetically, "Only enough change for one today." "Oh well, make it black," was Liz's response. I kept quiet and watched.

"You got a good girl there, Mum. We watch out for her on these streets."

This was a scenario that obviously happened every morning and I had no idea what was going on.

The waitress returned with a black coffee. My daughter didn't drink coffee and would not have considered having it black. Oblivious to my puzzlement, she opened the door and stepped out. The same man was still asleep on the doorstep. Liz bent down, gently shook his shoulder and spoke his name. He opened his eyes and looked up.

"Here's your coffee, just the way you like it."

I watched, momentarily paralyzed, as my daughter continued down the sidewalk. The man looked up at me, sizing me up instantly, reading both family resemblance and fear in my face. He shook his finger at me and said, in a voice still slurred by sleep, "You got a good girl there, Mum. We watch out for her on these streets."

The very people I had been worrying about were my daughter's guardian angels! Where I had seen potential trouble, she had seen God. That's pure of heart.

When I caught up with her, I asked, "What was that about?" "Oh, the coffee? Do you remember when I told you how much it hurt me to see so many homeless people on the streets? Do you remember what you told me? You said to do one thing, and do it faithfully. I do coffee."

"I do coffee."

I never did point out the dangers
of the city to my daughter.

My older sister had shared a similar experience with
me. She had volunteered for some time at the Dorothy
Day Catholic Worker House in New York City. On one
particular day, she had missed her subway stop and got
off in the middle of the poorest, most violent section of
Harlem. As she started her walk back north, a man began
following her. Nervously, she had increased her pace; the
man increased his. People watched from rundown porch-
es and balconies, but no one offered to help. Suddenly, a
male voice called out, "Leave her alone. She's from the
Worker." The man following her backed off. As she continued the several blocks north to the Worker soup
kitchen, the word went ahead of her, passing from porch
to porch, "Leave her alone. She's from the Worker."

The *Kabbalah* would tell us that when we see and bless
the Holy in the other, we are calling forth that goodness
by affirming the godlife within. Rachel Naomi Remen
says, "When we recognize the spark of God in others, we
blow on it with our attention and strengthen it, no matter how deeply it has been buried or for how long. When
we bless someone, we touch the unborn goodness in
them and wish it well."

When we are pure of heart, we see God.

God of Truth, give me the purity of heart
that sees beyond the external and discovers
the spark of the Holy hidden in everyone I meet.
Let their goodness and truth be a source of light
in my own life and the lives of all I touch.

A Blessing of Wisdom

Blessed are the peacemakers,
for they shall be called the children of God.

His name was Nicodemus. He was a pharisee, a learned man of God. He had probably heard Jesus preaching in the temple precincts. He was troubled by this young upstart whose interpretation of the sacred texts was so decidedly different from what he

Nicodemus was a tolerant man.

had spent his whole life studying. And he was curious.

Something rang true in the young rabbi's message, and yet, in so many ways, it was outside everything Nicodemus had been taught to believe. Not exactly contradictory, just totally different, as if the young rabbi was viewing the same religious history from a totally different perspective. He had not discarded the law, or the rituals that were so much a part of life for Nicodemus; he had placed them in a different context, giving them a different emphasis.

The other pharisees had condemned Jesus. He had no training, no schooling with the great rabbis. But Nicodemus was a tolerant man. Like the great Gamaleil, who would come later, he hesitated to condemn what might be from God. Yet, he did not want to risk being rejected by his peers, especially before he had determined for himself the truth of the message of the young rabbi.

And so he came quietly, by night, to delve into the mind of the man who had so angered his colleagues and so challenged himself. It is not hard to picture the two of them, sitting by candlelight, sharing a bottle of cheap wine and a loaf of bread. And arguing. For the good Jew, this discursive conversation is a form of prayer.

For every statement of Jesus, Nicodemus had another question.

"Unless a man be born again..."
"How can this be possible..."
(John 3:1–21).

> No one ever succeeded in "making" peace with guns.

It was a typical rabbinic discussion and it probably lasted the whole night. Not until the end of the gospel do we know the result of the discussion. After the crucifixion, it is Nicodemus who comes with Joseph of Aramathea to claim the body of Jesus and prepare it for burial. Nicodemus had discovered room within his own code of belief for a completely different outlook, and in the face of possible persecution, he acted on it.

Peacemaking is another one of the more badly misunderstood blessings. There is a great difference between peacemaking and peacekeeping. Peacekeeping can be done with weapons; it is possible to have "peacekeeping forces," as contradictory as the two words sound. No one, however, ever succeeded in "making" peace with guns.

The peacemakers are the ones who are not so convinced of their own truth that they are unable to see the truth of another. They do not have to make the other wrong in order to believe they are right. The peacemakers are willing to entertain the idea that the truth might be bigger than their own particular piece of it.

Truth is far more than any one of us can grasp.

As part of my graduate studies in the mid 1970s, I took a course on the documents of Vatican II with one of the *periti* (assistant theologians) who had been part of the council. He shared with us the fact that when *Lumen Gentium* was being written, the council fathers argued for weeks about the phrase "the truth exists in the Catholic Church." Conservatives felt it was the only way to explain the special relationship the Catholic Church has always believed it had with revelation. The moderates felt that the use of the word "exists" would alienate the other Christian churches and this was intended to be an ecumenical council. The fathers finally agreed on a phrase which can only be translated as "the truth subsists in the Catholic Church."

After struggling through the encyclical and reading the outside arguments, I decided on my own solution to the issue. The problem was not in verb "exists," the problem was in the subject of the sentence. If, instead of saying "the truth exists in the Catholic Church" they had simply said, "the Catholic Church exists in the truth" it would have solved the problem. If we believe that God is truth, none of us should have any difficulty believing that Truth is far more than any one of us can grasp. I suspect it is the same thing Sam Keen was saying in *Apology for Wonder* when he wrote: "Mysteries are not truths that lie beyond us: they are truths that comprehend us."

Nicodemus was struggling with the truth of his religion. His response was not to attack the position of Jesus or to defend his own position, but to question, to broaden his understanding, to find room in his truth for the truth of another.

There is another little-spoken-of disciple in scripture whom I believe is a peacemaker. His name is Nathaniel, sometimes called Bartholomew, the friend of Philip.

Philip heard about Jesus from Andrew, who was from his hometown. Later scriptures suggest to us that Philip was impulsive, warm, approachable, and probably young. It was Philip to whom Jesus turned when the multitude needed to be fed (John 6:5). It was Philip whom the Greeks approached when they wanted to gain access to Jesus (John 12:21). And Philip who worried aloud that they would not be able to follow Jesus if they did not know where he was going (John 12:21).

It is not hard to picture this young man running to his friend Nathaniel, and proclaiming that they had found the Messiah. Something in Nathaniel's answer would lead us to suspect it was not the first time that Philip had made outlandish claims for some new rabbi or revolutionary leader he had discovered. Nathaniel's response is

Peacemakers are open to the truth of others.

not as cynical as it sounds. It was probably made somewhat tongue in cheek to remind Philip of all the wild goose chases he had called Nathaniel to pursue.

"Can anything good come out of Nazareth?" (John 1:46).

Despite his own incredulity, he accepts Philip's invitation to "Come and see," probably more out of love for his friend than out of any kind of personal conviction. Yet, he is obviously open to what he might find. No matter how many times he may have been given good reason to doubt Philip, he is still willing to be open to the possibility of a truth that seems almost beyond comprehension, a Messiah from Nazareth.

It is this openness that Jesus recognizes as Nathaniel approaches him: "Here is an Israelite in whom there is no deceit" (John 1:47)

The peacemakers. Those who are open to the truth of others, even when it challenges their own truth. Theirs is a gift of true wisdom.

I have discovered, much to my own surprise, that my son is our peacemaker. Often in families, we think of the peacemaker as the person who is always trying to calm the waters, put a lid on things, and keep problems from erupting. This is not truly peacemaking; it is peacekeeping.

While our son has always been the gentlest of souls, the most even-tempered of our three, he would never be the one to squelch an argument. The simple truth of the matter is that my son could argue with anyone about anything, and usually does.

When he purchased his first real home, a postage stamp condo in downtown Boston, he called at least three times a week for advice. Like Nicodemus, those calls came late at night, without the benefit of the bottle of wine. He would ask about anything from relationships in his workplace to blinds for his windows. And when I would offer my advice, he would argue with it.

Finally, one night, exhausted by his persistence, I told him not to ask any more. I was not going to give him any more advice.

"Why not?" he asked, somewhat dismayed and horrified by my response.

"Because you don't listen," I responded in frustration.

"What are you talking about, Mom? I listen to you more than I listen to anyone!"

"No, you don't," I said wearily. "You argue."

"But that's how I listen!" he insisted emphatically.

While I laughed until the tears came, he explained himself.

We should learn to wait before what we know not, hoping to gain time and space sufficient to speak without lying.

"When I ask you your opinion, you tell me what you think. Now I have what you think and what I think. If I argue with what you think, you give me five reasons why you think it. And if I argue with each of those five reasons, you give me five more reasons for each of them. Now I have thirty reasons why you think what you do. And I can use them to make a good decision."

This is the argument of the peacemaker. It is not the contentious arguing of those who are trying to explain or justify themselves and their actions. The peacemakers do not argue to convince us of their truth, but that we can convince them of ours. "Persuade me. Broaden my truth, enliven my vision with your own particular piece of reality." As my son would point out, it's how they listen.

It is the listening that is essential, the listening that marks this as more than argument, the listening that leads to wisdom. And when the need to explain ourselves and our position is greatest, then the listening demands total silence.

In the wake of September 11, writing "A Pacifist Response" in *Walking with God in a Fragile World*, Stanley

Hauerwas states: "September 11 creates and requires a kind of silence. We desperately want to 'explain' what happened. Explanation domesticates terror, making it part of 'our' world. I believe attempts to explain must be resisted. Rather, we should learn to wait before what we know not, hoping to gain time and space sufficient to speak without lying. I should like to think pacifism names the habit and community necessary to gain the time and place that is an alternative to revenge."

Wisdom does not lie solely in our own truth, or in the other's, but precisely in the effort to communicate, to listen, to respect, and to understand.

Sophia, God of Wisdom, open my ears to listen like a disciple. Keep me faithful in the struggle to be attentive to the truth of others. Transform my openness to wisdom, and wisdom to peace, for my family, our church, and our world.

A Blessing of Shadows

Blessed are they who suffer persecution for justice sake, theirs is the kingdom of heaven.

It doesn't sound like a blessing! Perhaps it is not so much a gift as it is the consequence of living our own particular blessing. Anyone who lives life as a blessing, who tries to be a blessing to others, will be persecuted.

Oh, we probably won't be thrown to the lions, or even thrown out of the synagogues, as Jesus suggested. The persecution will be much more subtle and insidious. It will deny us the opportunity to see ourselves as martyrs while it eats away at our courage and conviction.

Our persecutors are our critics, our enemies, all those threatened by our attempt to live life authentically. When we are willing to listen, our enemies actually tell us far more about ourselves than our friends. Those who agree with us never really challenge us to rethink our position, justify our choices, stand up for what we most believe in. It is our critics who give us that gift.

I never truly understood what it meant to be Roman Catholic until I spent four summers teaching a course on spirituality at the University of Judaism. My doctoral work was at a Protestant seminary, but my classmates and I had managed to agree on most things. I could say "Baptism" or "Eucharist" and they would say "Yes, yes, we believe in that." We actually believed very different things about those concepts, but their very agreement kept me from clearly explaining what I meant when I said those words.

It was my Jewish friends and colleagues who said "No way!" who forced me to clarify what I was celebrating in those rituals, who made me articulate what I believed when I said "Amen." Every tenet of the creed took on more meaning when seen in contrast, not to their unbelief, but to their differing belief.

Our critics,
and even
our enemies,
often give us
the greatest
insights into
ourselves.

Those who disagree, our critics, and even our enemies, often give us the greatest insights into ourselves. If you have read through this book and are still wondering, "What is my blessing?" listen to your critics.

Do they accuse you of being a "soft touch?" Do they offer to sell you bridges in Brooklyn, or wherever those symbolic bridges exist in other parts of the country? It could be that you are the poor in spirit, one whose greatest joy is in giving. Your critics cannot comprehend that your willingness to give is not dependent on the gratitude of the other. It flows from your own gratitude for all you have been given.

Perhaps you are easily moved to tears and are constantly being told to develop "a tougher skin." "You can't let things get to you." You could be a blessed mourner.

Maybe you are the meek, one of those people of courage who speak the truth to power. Your critics accuse you of always sticking your neck out, banging your head against the same stone walls. But in your world, there is nothing you are not willing to lose in the effort to gain all that you believe can be gained by speaking out with courage.

Perhaps you have been told that the little bit you can do will never be enough to make a difference. One fam-

Are you accused of being a doormat because you refuse to enact vengeance?

ily refusing to use paper napkins, in one small town in Connecticut, is simply not going to have an impact on deforestation. Your critics insist you are foolish to expend your time and your energy on such a small gesture. But your detractors will never understand that just because you can't do enough, this will never keep you from doing what you can. This is your hunger and thirst for justice.

Are you the merciful? A recent survey done in anticipation of Connecticut's execution of Michael Ross indicated that 67% of Catholics in that state believed in the death penalty. Surveys done in earlier years had reported a much lower percentage, but that was when the person on death row and his victims were not so well known to so many, and the issue wasn't as personal as the Michael Ross case became. When the crime, the insult, the theft, the rejection, affect you intimately, are you accused of being a doormat because you refuse to enact vengeance?

Perhaps you are the pure of heart. Your critics laugh at what they call your naïvité, but it is not foolishness that leads you into trust, and into relationships with people whom others scorn or avoid. It is insight into the heart of the other. It is there, in relationship, that you are most apt to find God.

Are you a peacemaker? Are you the one who is willing to argue with the other's point of view until you reach the place where it enlarges your own? Do your critics condemn you for arguing with everything, then failing to fight for your own "rightness"?

If your critics have not taught you your gift, perhaps it is your own internal critic that might offer the insight. Many of us raised Catholic grew up with the belief that the only way to become holy and to live a deeply happy and contented life was to rid ourselves of all our faults and failings. My Catholic school training taught me to examine my conscience twice a day, once for the general faults and failings I had fallen into, and then a "particular examen" of the specific fault I was working on expunging from my inner self.

After years of failure and not a little self-hate, I have found great comfort in the words of Tom Stella: "I have come to realize that I can only become who I am meant to be by accepting who I happen to be, namely, the complex mix of contradictory needs and urges....We are light and darkness, virtue and vice, saintly and sinful....The changes that might make us more peaceful within and better able to live peaceably with others are more likely to come about not by a process of elimination, but by one of integration."

In exploring Stella's idea of integration, I have discovered that my greatest faults are often the shadow side of my greatest gifts. The passion that can push me into a murderous desire for revenge is the same passion that pushes me to proclaim the good news of forgiveness to others who have known that same rage. I am shadow and light, and, just as it is throughout all of nature, shadows are the indicators of light. When the shadows stretch before us, the light is at our backs. Tom Stella invited me to let the shadows be a reminder to turn around and seek the light.

I suspect, in the acceptance of both shadow and light, we can discover the blessing we are. The greatest obstacle to living our blessing is our stubborn holding on to our limits, our unwillingness to believe we are gifted, people of light.

"Can you believe in me, the way that I believe in you?"

It is easier to turn the blessings into commandments and berate ourselves for not living up to them. That fits in with our cultural need to be in control, to be working out our salvation. There is something a little fearful in

> In the acceptance of both shadow and light, we can discover the blessing we are.

There is something a little fearful in the idea that it is all gift.

the idea that it is all gift, that we have been given all we need to be blessing for the world, that we are the spark of the Holy.

And Jesus sings: "Can you believe in me, the way that I believe in you?"

There is a story from my teenage years that I have shared before, in writing and talks, but I am sharing it again, as it really belongs here. I was fifteen at the time, and having one of those horrible days that only fifteen-year-old girls can have. It was a bad hair day, my acne was in outright rebellion, and my uniform blouse seemed to emphasize the lack of anything underneath it to give it form. I stood in front of our bathroom mirror, saying out loud, repeatedly, "You are so ugly!"

My mom happened to be walking by the door and caught my tirade. She stepped inside, laid a hand on my shoulder, and said calmly, "How dare you criticize my handiwork!"

In the years since, there have been many times when I have heard God speaking in my mother's voice, saying the very same thing.

"How dare you criticize my handiwork. When will you ever believe in me the way that I believe in you?"

We are gifted; we are blessed. It is in seeking to live our blessing with integrity, to be a blessing to all we touch, that we become radiant. All those who wander into our light can see their own lives a little more clearly in our presence.

Rejoice, and be glad. Ours is the kingdom of God.

Conclusion

I don't want white lines
    down the middle of my streets.
My streets
    like my highways
    have no edges,
    just as they have
    no beginning
    or end.
          —Dom Helder Camara

I have spent the last ten years searching scripture for people to name the blessings I have come to understand as the heart of the sermon on the mount. I have read and reread the gospel stories, giving myself the freedom to play them out differently, trying blessings on parables and persons, listening to the stories their lives awaken in my heart.

I hope you will disagree with at least some of my choices. I hope it will prompt you to go to the scriptures yourself, in search of your own people of blessing. And then I

I keep bumping into the Holy in a thousand unexpected places.

hope you will write and argue with me. Remember, I am the mother of a peacemaker; I have learned how to listen through arguing.

My search has overflowed into life and I have found myself watching the people in my family circle, the people with whom I work, the people I meet on my travels, with a new awareness. Realizing I will never know the others' truth with certitude, it is still fun to guess at the particular blessing with which they bless the world, and to recognize the way in which their being blesses me.

In the process, something extraordinary has happened to me. I keep bumping into the Holy in a thousand unexpected places.

And so this search for blessings that began on a small boat on a fog-shrouded sea, has become a journey with no clear boundaries. My son once described his graduation from college as coming to "the place on the edge of town where the sidewalks run out." Like my son, I have found there are no more sidewalks, my streets no longer have edges.

What was once clearly defined for me as the Holy, has expanded infinitely into the realm of mystery.

I am learning to walk barefoot, on holy ground.

For Discussion

I suspect this will be a book that adapts well to book club discussions. It has been a frequent topic of presentations and retreats for me, and I never speak about it without people wanting to discuss, question, challenge my choices, as well as add their own. For this reason, I am including discussion questions to jumpstart that conversation.

Chapter 1

- Were you taught the beatitudes as a child?

- What were you taught about them?

- What did you learn about the idea of blessing?

- Do you have any new insights on the topic after reading this chapter?

- What do you think about the possibility that Jesus meant these words as a blessing, a recognition of the holiness of the people?

Chapter 2

- When have you experienced a "consciousness of abundance," and how did it make you feel?

- Who was the most hospitable person you have ever known?

- Can you name someone from Scripture or contemporary life whom you believe is poor in spirit?

Chapter 3

- What do you think makes a person a blessed mourner?
- Read the other Martha and Mary story in Luke 10:38–42. What does this story tell you about their friendship with Jesus? What do you think is Mary's blessing?
- In the wake of 9/11, our country had difficulty finding collective ways to mourn our loss. What were some of the symbols and rituals we chose for our mourning?
- Can you name someone from Scripture or contemporary life whom you consider a blessed mourner?

Chapter 4

- What do you think of when you think of meekness?
- Do you think the author has grounds for her definition?
- Can you name someone from Scripture or contemporary life whom you believe is meek?

Chapter 5

- Some have suggested that I confuse meekness with justice. How do you see these two beatitudes as different?

- Do you believe it is possible to have a "hunger and thirst" for justice that is even stronger than the universal call to justice in the gospels?

- Can you name someone from Scripture or contemporary life whom you believe is one of the people who hungers and thirsts for justice?

Chapter 6

- When have you been shown mercy?

- When have you been moved to act with mercy?

- Do you think the elder brother in the prodigal son story joined the party? Why? Why not?

- Can you name someone from Scripture or contemporary life who is merciful?

Chapter 7

- Before reading this chapter, how would you have defined the pure of heart?

- Now, if you had to describe the meaning of "pure of heart," how would you do it?

- Can you name someone from Scripture or contemporary life who is pure of heart?

Chapter 8

- What do you believe is necessary in order to make peace?

- Are there nations in today's world that you consider more "peacemaking" than others? Why?

- Can you suggest any ways we can work toward peace in our world?

- Can you name someone from Scripture or contemporary life who is a peacemaker?

Chapter 9

- What is your blessing?

- What will it take for you to believe, the way that God believes in you?

Resources

(in order cited)

My Grandfather's Blessings: Stories of Strength, Refuge, and Belonging, Rachel Naomi Remen. New York: Riverhead Books, 2000, pp. 2-3, 110, 198.

The Complete Book of Jewish Observance: A Practical Manual for the Modern Jew, Leo Trepp. New York: Behram House Books, 1980, p. 44.

Everyday Simplicity, Robert Wicks. Notre Dame, IN: Ave Maria Press, 2000, p. 52.

Called to Question: A Spiritual Memoir, Joan Chittister, OSB. New York: Sheed and Ward, 2004, p. 144.

The Majesty of the Law: Reflections of a Supreme Court Justice, Sandra Day O'Connor. New York: Random House, 2003, p. 133.

Writing in the Dust: After September 11, Rowan Williams. Grand Rapids, MI: Wm Erdmans Publishing Company, 2002, pp. 25, 115.

Scarred by Struggle, Transformed by Hope, Joan Chittister, OSB. Grand Rapids, MI: Wm Erdmans Publishing Company, 2000, pp. 51, 145.

Apology for Wonder, Sam Keen. New York: Harper and Row, 1969, pp. 24-25.

Walking with God in a Fragile World, Stanley Hauerwas. New York: Rowan Littlefield, 2003, pp. 121-122.

A Thousand Reasons for Living, Dom Helder Camara. Philadelphia: Fortress Press, 1981, p. 61.